WAY TO GO!

Sports Poems
by Lillian Morrison

Illustrations by Susan Spellman

Wordsong · Boyds Mills Press

For my brother, Milton,
my childhood pal and sports partner—L. M.

For my three daughters,
who all "move the body with grace"—S. S.

The following poems have been previously published:

"At the Tennis Clinic" (previously titled "Tennis Clinic"), "Completed Pass" (previously titled "Passing Fair"), "I Love All Gravity Defiers," "In the beginning was the," "Nine Triads," "On Our Bikes," "Sailing, Sailing," "The Sidewalk Racer," "The Spearthrower," "The Sprinters," "Surf," "The Surfer," and "The Women's 400 Meters" in *The Sidewalk Racer and Other Poems of Sports and Motion.* Copyright © 1965, 1967, 1968, 1977 by Lillian Morrison.

"Basketball Players," "Bike Tour," "Canoe and Ducks," "Downhill Racer," "The Finish Line," "Gold Medalist," "The 100 Meters," "Slalom Skier," "The Speed Skaters," and "Two to Nothing" in *The Break Dance Kids.* Copyright © 1985 by Lillian Morrison.

"Solitary Practice" (under the pseudonym William Revas) and "The Women's Team at L. Bamberger & Co." in *Slam Dunk.* Copyright © 1995 by Lillian Morrison.

"Seascape" (previously titled "Sea Song") in *Miranda's Music.* Copyright © 1968 by Lillian Morrison.

"Fan Valentines" was first published in *Fan: A Baseball Magazine.*

Text copyright © 2001 by Lillian Morrison
Illustrations copyright © 2001 by Susan Spellman
All rights reserved

Wordsong
An Imprint of Boyds Mills Press, Inc.
A Highlights Company
815 Church Street
Honesdale, Pennsylvania 18431
Printed in China

U.S. Cataloging-in-Publication Data
    (Library of Congress Standards)

Morrison, Lillian.
    Way to go : sports poems / by Lillian Morrison ;
illustrations by Susan Spellman.—1st ed.
[48] p. : ill. ; cm.
Includes index.
Summary: Verses describe the joy and excitement of sports
such as basketball, skiing, sprinting, biking, and surfing.
ISBN 978-1-59078-481-5
1. Sports—Poetry. 2. American poetry. I. Spellman,
Susan. II. Title.
811.54 21 2001 CIP   AC
00-107720

First Boyds Mills Press paperback edition, 2006
Book designed by Jason Thorne
The text of this book is set in 12-point Palatino.

www.boydsmillspress.com

10 9 8 7 6 5 4 3 2 1

CONTENTS

WITH A BALL

Basketball Players 6
Solitary Practice 6
The Women's Team at
  L. Bamberger & Co. 7
At the Tennis Clinic 8
Tennis Paradox 8
The Ace at Match Point 9
Two to Nothing 10
The Homer 11
The Bunt with a Man on First . 12
Fan Valentines 13
Preventing a Steal 13
In the beginning was the 14
Completed Pass 14
High School Soccer Player,
  or Kickin' It 15

WINTER WORLD

Downhill Racer 18
Slalom Skier 19
The Joys of Snowboarding 20
The Snowboarder 21
Nordic Skier, or Beginner in the
  Backcountry 22
Cross-country Elation 23
The Speed Skaters 24

TRACK AND FIELD

The Sprinters 26
The 100 Meters 27
The Women's 400 Meters 27
Racers 28
The Finish Line 28
The Spearthrower 29

ON WHEELS

Bike Tour 32
On Our Bikes 32
The Sidewalk Racer,
  or On the Skateboard 33
The Rollerblader 34
In-line Variation 35

ON THE WATER

Seascape 38
Short Voyage 39
Sailing, Sailing 40
Joyrider 41
The Surfer 41
Surf 42
Canoe and Ducks 42

THE SPIRIT OF SPORT

I Love All Gravity Defiers 44
Gold Medalist 45
Nine Triads (After the Irish,
  9th Century) 46

Index of Titles and
First Lines 48

With a Ball

Basketball Players

It's possible for a player
to jump because he's happy,
but it's more likely that he's
happy because he's jumping.
—Bill Russell in *Second Wind*

When we're happy,
we jump for joy.
Basketball players
jump as ploy
to get the ball
or net the ball.
Jump! Slam-dunk!
Come down, splatSPLAT.
They get *their* joy
out of that.
And they like the sound,
as well as the soaring,
as they pound down the floor,
of the crowd roaring.

Solitary Practice

Dribble, dribble and shoot.
I just dunked a beaut.
Fast break down the floor,
Fake a pass, shoot once more.
In again. Perfect aim.
Why can't I do this in a game?

The Women's Team
at L. Bamberger & Co.

Our best forward
wasn't very tall
but made up for it
in speed, spunk, and
spring in the knees.
She could almost slam-dunk.
Proud, in our snazzy
silver shorts, maroon tops,
we ran and sweated
in those drafty gyms
(seats mostly empty)
somehow always playing
against bigger, rougher teams,
tough girls who shoved
and elbowed, but Maggie's
fakes and pivots, charges
down the floor, lay-ups,
jumpers, one-handers
would fire us up, and the
few times we did win,
the bare locker rooms,
as we showered and dressed,
rang with our rejoicing
and when we emerged, heading
for the bus, each of us
at least two inches taller,
the frosty air outside
seemed to greet us with kisses.

At the Tennis Clinic

There was a young man from Port Jervis
Who developed a marvelous service
But was sorry he learned it
For if someone returned it
It made him impossibly nervous.

Tennis Paradox

Though it seems rather strange
It's true from coast to coast:
When he bests you in a love match,
You hate the guy the most.

The Ace at Match Point

She's serving now, delivers.
Let! The net cord shivers.
Next serve. What awesome power!
100 miles an hour.
No time to even swing.
No time for anything.
The ball whizzed past. Don't cry.
Just kiss this match good-bye.

Two to Nothing

Catcher, the ball caller
  knees bent, squatting;
Pitcher, a slider guider
  peering, plotting.
First up, a pop-up
  hung his head, spit.
Next up, a bloop looper
  got a cheap hit.
Then came a bunt dumper
  out at first base
  (a runner with pep
  but out by a step).
Then came the power—
  the big number one
slammed a low pitch
  for a towering home run.

The Homer

It was a humid afternoon
And one I won't forget so soon.

Under the broiling, baking sun
I hit my first real-life home run.

I gripped the bat with sweaty hands
And FWACK! What cheering in the stands!

It felt so good to round the bases
And look at all the happy faces

And from the bench, head in a whirl,
I heard Dad yelling, "That's my girl!"

The Bunt with a Man on First

Among hits, the bunt
is the runt. The bat
blunts the brunt of the
ball. Then there's the
charge up front to snag
it as the batter races
to first, hoping for a
safe call on the throw
and the runner on first
moves to second. This
time it worked really
fine. Johnny laid one
down the line. And we
feel that tingle of
sweet satisfaction for
the adroit bit of action
that made this bunt single.

Fan Valentines

Yours till the pinch hits
Yours till the seventh inning stretches
Yours till the pennant races
Yours till the pop flies
Yours till the home runs
Yours till the line drives
Yours till the double plays
Yours till the batters box

Preventing a Steal

Be sure to tag
before the runner
gets any part
of his anatomy
on the bag.
A fingertip
can trip you up,
so be alert
as he hits the dirt
and slides—
avoid those spikes
and TAG!
Well, is he safe?
The ump decides.

In the beginning was the

Kickoff.
The ball flew
looping down true
into the end zone
where it was snagged,
neatly hugged
by a swivel-hipped back
who ran up the field
and was smeared.

The game has begun.
The game has been won.
The game goes on.
Long live the game.
Gather and lock
tackle and block
move, move,
around the arena
and always the beautiful
trajectories.

Completed Pass

There is nothing more pleasing
than to pluck a long forward pass
from the air
on a field of grass
except perhaps
to have thrown the pass.

High School Soccer Player,
or Kickin' It

I don't have the techniques of Pelé,
I don't have a World Cup dream
But I love to kick that soccer ball
All for the good of my team.

Kickin' it, kickin' it, kickin' it—
This is the life for me:
Sprinting and sweating and passing the ball,
Aiming for victory,

Slide-tackling my opponent,
Finding that opportune hole
And slamming a shot bang into the net
As the referee signals, "GOAL!!!"

Winter World

Downhill Racer

Over the snow-covered
slopes and dips she
swoops flies skis
sighing skims bumps
and hollows rounding
the turns to race the
reeling clock zips
down down rocking
for the last speck
of speed *uh-oh!*
almost tumbles re-
covers now hunched
  for the long
      schuss
          in.

Did she win?
A hundredth of a second
could make the difference.
She smiles in spite of
fears removes goggles.
The mountainsides
reverberate with cheers.

Slalom Skier

Snow dancer
    slant dancer
        adept in the art
     of swiveling
  he tangos down
through the tall stalks
    with their fluttering flags
       not one is missed
   then does the twist
     as the gates
      come closer
    and closer together
      smoothly angles
  in and out
      threads each one
  until the final
    hissing glide
     and the run is done.

The Joys of Snowboarding

I laugh out loud
As I float through powder,
Float through the fluffy snow.

I do a front flip
And laugh even louder.
Big air—the way to go!

Down to the lift
Then up again,
Making this board behave

As I speed down the hill
In graceful arcs,
Surfing the winter wave.

The Snowboarder

Snow, soft, white
In the morning light
Takeoff! And I'm in flight.

Down the hill
In the vivid chill
Bumps, jumps, and nary a spill.

Never knew I could
Feel so good—
Just me on a four-foot piece of wood.

Nordic Skier,
or
Beginner in the Backcountry

I'm a two-legged schooner in the Arctic,
An explorer on a trek.
My name will go down in history.
(That's cold sweat on my neck.)

Even though my nose is running
And the sun is blinding my eyes
And my backpack is rather heavy
I'm getting good exercise.

If I go too fast, I just flop down
So I'm often buried in snow,
But this forest of white is magical.
I'm ready again. Let's go!

Cross-country Elation

I enter a winter landscape—
Kick glide, kick glide, kick glide.
In this silent world of snow
I have found my stride.

I plot my course. I move
Past vistas that astound me.
Forward track, inhaling deep
The sharp air all around me.

I love this smell of snow,
The soft hiss of my skis.
I greet a passing red-tailed hawk
Above me in the breeze.

Now I'm in perfect rhythm.
Somehow all care has flown.
So this is the famous runner's high!
Bliss. I'm in the zone.

The Speed Skaters

When the skaters push
with powerful thighs
round the rink
leaning far forward
streamlined for speed,
do they think,
"This may be thin ice"?
Oh no. Air is the
adversary, and time,
suits are skintight
the better for swimming
and their long arms
swing in great arcs.

Orangutans of grace
alien creatures
freed from normal laws
of human speed
they offer us the gift
of their slick
self-propelling.
Now, for the moment,
we too are swift
beyond barriers.

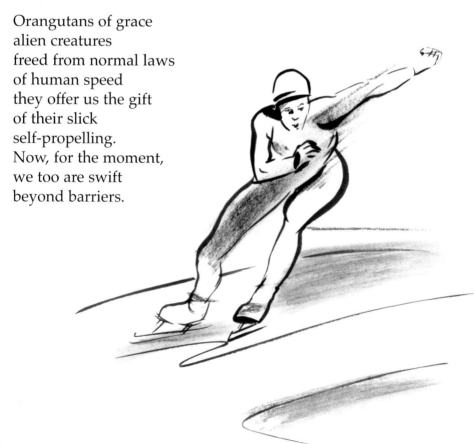

Track and Field

The Sprinters

The gun explodes them.
Pummeling, pistoning they fly
In time's face.
A go at the limit
A terrible try
To smash the ticking glass,
Outpace the beat
That runs, that streaks away
Tireless, and faster than they.

Beside ourselves
(It is for us they run!)
We shout and pound the stands
For one to win
Loving him, whose hard
Grace-driven stride
Most mocks the clock
And almost breaks the bands
Which lock us in.

The 100 Meters

Sprung from the starting blocks
they punch down the stretch
fly   gulp air as the stride
quickens as arms flail try
try   the agonized moment
drops.

Beyond the finish line
they jog a little,
bend over, saunter off,
the winner's arm round the neck
of a glad supporter.

Later, hands on hips,
those springing limbs
now leaning at ease,
they rest on the laurels
of noble exertion
and listen for the time.

The Women's 400 Meters

Skittish,
they flex knees, drum heels and
shiver at the starting line

waiting the gun
to pour them over the stretch
like a breaking wave.

Bang! they're off
careening down the lanes,
each chased by her own bright tiger.

Racers

On the track, on the trail,
In the park, on the hill,
Why do we race, the wind in our faces?

Pacing ourselves,
Having practiced, prepared,
Is it merely to come in first?

Winners or losers,
We reach as we run.
We race to embrace the world.

The Finish Line

There is the finish line
but the runner can cross it
again and again.

She will not be finished
for a long time
but always beginning

getting ready and set
for another GO!
a better finish.

The Spearthrower

She walks alone
to the edge of the park
and throws into
the bullying dark
her javelin
of light,
her singing sign
her signed song
that the runner may run
far and long
her quick laps
on the curving track
that the sprinter surge
and the hurdler leap
that the vaulter soar,
clear the highest bar,
and the discus fly
as the great crowds cry
to their heroines
Come on!

On Wheels

Bike Tour

Spray and early sun,
misty clean morning,
as row on row of flat
breakers roll in, and
a lone surfer rides them
in the white light of dawn.

We breathe deep and watch.
How good the oranges taste
before we mount our bikes
again, dawn behind us,
to take on noon and night,
pores open, head on.

On Our Bikes

The roads to the beach
                are winding
  we glide down
          breeze-whipped
curving
        past hills of sand
  pedal and coast
                through wide smell of the sea
              old familiar sunfeel
    windwallop.

Race you to the water's edge!

The Sidewalk Racer,
or On the Skateboard

Skimming
an asphalt sea
I swerve, I curve, I
sway; I speed to whirring
sound an inch above the
ground; I'm the sailor
and the sail, I'm the
driver and the wheel
I'm the one and only
single engine
human auto
mobile

The Rollerblader

He puts on his helmet,
He fastens his pads.
No more skating on the old-time quads.
He's an in-line skater,
He's a Rollerblader
Gliding all over the town.

He's an acrobat
On the toughest rails.
He's a leader on the hilly trails.
So take to your heels
When he's on wheels
Or his speed will mow you down.

In-line Variation

Don't need any snow,
Don't need any ice,
Just give me two poles and a hill

And away I go
On my in-line skates
Feeling the skier's thrill.

My name is Glenda
And I like to pretend
That I'm an Olympian, too

As I weave side to side
Slaloming down
The hilly avenue.

On the Water

Seascape

Rich in the rocking bays,
Fat in the lapping waves,
Little yachts go skimming nip and tuck.

Trim in the snapping sun,
One with the swooping gulls,
Slim patrician sailboats dip and duck.

Now higher than the sky,
(Wind slapping swiftly by)
Pure and pouring water lifts them up.

Short Voyage

The breeze has turned
the surface of the bay
from silk to crepe de chine.

The ducks are bobbing
as they float
on the aqua marine.

Now the sea
is *really* choppy.
The wind is blowing keener.

I THINK IT'S TIME
TO HEAD OUR BOAT
BACK TO THE MARINA!

Sailing, Sailing

(Lines written to keep the mind off incipient seasickness)

There is no impeding
That proceeding,
No deflating
That undulating
Or overthrowing
The to-and-froing
Or undoing
The fro-and-toing,
That silky insisting
Never desisting,
That creasing, uncreasing
Never ceasing,
No deterrence
To the recurrence,
No cessation
To the pulsation,
No stopping the dropping
Of the wave,
The plopping, slopping
Of the foam.
We brave it
Afloat in a boat
On the perpetual
Wet-you-all
(No controlling that rolling)
Motion
Hasten, Jason
Of the ocean.
Get the basin.

Joyrider

Storm-started
two thousand miles away,
her wave comes curling.

A connoisseur of crests,
she waits to catch it
then nips the moment

takes off, knees bent
and swaying, fast, fast
swoops in to shore.

No wipeout this time.
She wades and waits again
for the next ecstatic waltz on water.

The Surfer

He paddles out,
awaits his chosen wave,
the curling water
that will ride him in.
Spilling, it comes
and he's a water bird
in flight
for thirty seconds.

Surf

Waves want
to be wheels,
They jump for it
and fail
fall flat
like pole vaulters
and sprawl
arms outstretched
foam fingers
reaching.

Canoe and Ducks

In smooth single file
eight mergansers glide;
first in a circle
then in a row they
ride the water mirror.

Now they huddle,
now spread out, now
dip heads in the lake
without a splash;
then rise and shake
their feathers,
following the leader.

We watch the silent
aquacade. They
sail on one by one,
and, dipping paddles,
we glide as soundlessly,
the sun, now
dipping too and gone
below the horizon.

The Spirit of Sport

I Love All
Gravity Defiers

The vaulter suspended
on a slender pole
hangs in the air
before his fall.

The trapeze artist
tumbles through space
in split-second rescues
from the abyss.

Kids on swings
pumping to the sky
in a pendulum of pleasure,
fly.

Ski jumpers, speed-propelled,
extended in flight
loop down
to land upright.

Hail gravity defiers,
jumpers, broad and high
and all nonjumpers
who will not drop, who try.

Somersaulters
on the trampoline,
battered boxers
up at the count of nine.

Springboard athletes
jackknifing as they dive
and people who stand straight
and stay alive.

Gold Medalist

In all my endeavor
I wish to be ever
A straight arrow spearing
Just past the possible.

Nine Triads
(After the Irish, 9th Century)

Three grand arcs:
      the lift of the pole vaulter over the bar
      the golf ball's flight to the green
      the home run into the bleachers

Three pleasurable curves:
      the ice skater's figure eight
      the long cast of the fisherman
      the arched back of the gymnast

Three swishes that lift the heart:
      the basketball's spin through the net
      the skier's swoop down the snowpacked hill
      the diver's entry into the water

Three glides of satisfaction:
      the ice hockey forward's, after the goal
      the swimmer's turn at the end of the pool
      the finish of the bobsled run

Three swift arrivals to admire:
      the completed pass
      the arrow into the bull's-eye
      the sprinter at the tape

Three shots requiring skill:
    the slap shot
    the shot put
    the putt out

Three carriers of suspense:
    the place kick for a field goal
    the rim shot
    three balls and two strikes

Three vital sounds:
    the hunter's horn
    the starter's gun
    the bell for the end of the round

Three excellent wishes:
    to move the body with grace
    to fly without a machine
    to outrun time

Index of *Titles* and First Lines

Ace at Match Point, The 9
Among hits, the bunt 12
At the Tennis Clinic 8
Basketball Players 6
Be sure to tag 13
Bike Tour 32
Bunt with a Man on First, The 12
Canoe and Ducks 42
Catcher, the ball caller 10
Completed Pass 14
Cross-country Elation 23
Don't need any snow, ... 35
Downhill Racer 18
Dribble, dribble and shoot. 6
Fan Valentines 13
Finish Line, The 28
Gold Medalist 45
He paddles out, ... 41
He puts on his helmet, ... 34
High School Soccer Player, or Kickin' It 15
Homer, The 11
I don't have the techniques of Pelé, ... 15
I enter a winter landscape— 23
I laugh out loud 20
I Love All Gravity Defiers 44
I'm a two-legged schooner in the Arctic, . 22
In all my endeavor 45
In smooth single file 42
In the beginning was the 14
In the beginning was the 14
In-line Variation 35
It was a humid afternoon 11
Joyrider 41
Joys of Snowboarding, The 20
Nine Triads (After the Irish, 9th Century) . . . 46
Nordic Skier, or Beginner in the Backcountry . 22
On Our Bikes 32
On the track, on the trail, ... 28
100 Meters, The 27
Our best forward 7
Over the snow-covered 18
Preventing a Steal 13

Racers 28
Rich in the rocking bays, ... 38
Rollerblader, The 34
Sailing, Sailing 40
Seascape 38
She walks alone 29
She's serving now, delivers. 9
Short Voyage 39
Sidewalker Racer, The, or On the Skateboard . 33
Skimming 33
Skittish, ... 27
Slalom Skier 19
Snow dancer 19
Snow, soft, white 21
Snowboarder, The 21
Solitary Practice 6
Spearthrower, The 29
Speed Skaters, The 24
Spray and early sun, ... 32
Sprinters, The 26
Sprung from the starting blocks 27
Storm-started 41
Surf 42
Surfer, The 41
Tennis Paradox 8
The breeze has turned 39
The gun explodes them. 26
The roads to the beach 32
The vaulter suspended 44
There is no impeding 40
There is nothing more pleasing 14
There is the finish line 28
There was a young man from Port Jervis . . 8
Though it seems rather strange 8
Three grand arcs: 46
Two to Nothing 10
Waves want 42
When the skaters push 24
When we're happy, ... 6
Women's 400 Meters, The 27
Women's Team at L. Bamberger & Co., The . . . 7
Yours till the pinch hits 13